QATAR 2016 HUMAN RIGHTS REPORT

EXECUTIVE SUMMARY

Qatar is a constitutional monarchy in which Emir Sheikh Tamim bin Hamad Al Thani exercises full executive power. The constitution provides for hereditary rule by men in the emir's branch of the Al Thani family, which has ruled since 1868. The most recent elections were in 2015 for the Central Municipal Council, an advisory and consultative body; observers considered them free and fair.

Civilian authorities maintained effective control over security forces.

The principal human rights problems were the inability of citizens to choose their government in free and fair periodic elections, restriction of fundamental civil liberties, and denial of the rights of foreign workers. The monarch-appointed government prohibited organized political parties and restricted civil liberties, including freedoms of speech, press, and assembly and access to a fair trial for persons held under the Protection of Society Law and the Combating Terrorism Law.

Other continuing human rights concerns included restrictions on the freedoms of religion and movement, since migrant workers could not freely travel abroad. Legal, institutional, and cultural discrimination against women limited their participation in society. Trafficking in persons, primarily in the domestic worker and labor sectors, was a continuing problem. The noncitizen "bidoon" (stateless persons) who resided in the country with unresolved legal status experienced social discrimination.

The government took limited steps to prosecute those who committed abuses.

Section 1. Respect for the Integrity of the Person, Including Freedom from:

a. Arbitrary Deprivation of Life and other Unlawful or Politically Motivated Killings

There were no reports that the government or its agents committed arbitrary or unlawful killings during the year.

b. Disappearance

There were no reports of politically motivated disappearances.

c. Torture and Other Cruel, Inhuman, or Degrading Treatment or Punishment

The constitution and law prohibit torture and other inhuman or degrading treatment and punishment; the National Human Rights Committee (NHRC) investigated three allegations of torture and beatings by security forces in their last report but found no evidence to substantiate those claims.

The government interprets sharia as allowing corporal punishment for certain criminal offenses, including court-ordered flogging in cases of alcohol consumption and extramarital sex by Muslims. On past appeals, courts typically reduced this sentence to imprisonment or a fine. In June a court sentenced a Syrian man to 40 lashes for alcohol consumption and 100 lashes for illicit sex acts, although he eventually received only 50 lashes.

Prison and Detention Center Conditions

Aside from the Deportation Detention Center (DDC), prison conditions generally met international standards. The 2015 report of the NHRC stated that the committee paid 17 surprise visits to various detention and interrogation facilities across the country in 2015 and concluded that the facilities met international standards. The committee recommended that the Deportation Camp expand and undertake some health and safety improvements at the facility.

Physical Conditions: There were no reported serious shortcomings in the physical conditions provided to those incarcerated in the prison or detention centers.

Administration: No legal statute allows for ombudsmen to advocate for prisoners and detainees.

Independent Monitoring: The government permitted monitoring visits by independent human rights observers and international bodies to all facilities except the state security prison. The government routinely provided foreign diplomats access to state security prisoners at separate locations and did so during the year. Representatives from the NHRC conducted regular visits to all facilities.

d. Arbitrary Arrest or Detention

The constitution prohibits arbitrary arrest and detention, and the government usually observed these prohibitions. There were isolated reports that authorities arbitrarily arrested and detained some individuals. Authorities detained a group of Danish journalists while producing a news report on labor accommodations. Those detained alleged these detentions were arbitrary and intended to interfere with their investigations.

Authorities may detain individuals in the state security prison for indefinite periods under the Protection of Society Law and the Combating Terrorism Law. The government limited detention to two months, however, for all DDC detainees except those facing additional financial criminal charges. The processing time for deportations ranged from two days to 10 months. There were also reports that authorities delayed deportations up to 10 months in cases where detainees had to resolve financial delinquencies before they departed the country.

Role of the Police and Security Apparatus

The national police and state security forces maintain internal security. State security forces address internal threats such as terrorism, political disputes, cyberattacks, or espionage while the national police are the regular law enforcement body. The army is responsible for external security. Civilian authorities maintained effective control over the police under the Ministry of Interior, state security forces, which report directly to the emir, and military forces under the Ministry of Defense. The government employed effective mechanisms to investigate and punish abuse and corruption.

There were no reports of impunity of the security forces.

Arrest Procedures and Treatment of Detainees

Criminal law requires that persons be apprehended openly with warrants based on sufficient evidence and issued by a duly authorized official, be charged within 24 hours, and be brought before a court without undue delay, although the law empowers the judge investigating the case to extend the total detention period to six months before the case goes to court. The state security service may arrest and detain suspects for up to 30 days without referring them to the public prosecutor.

The law provides procedures that permit detention without charge for as long as 15 days, renewable for up to six months. The law permits an additional six months' detention without charge with the approval of the prime minister, who may extend the detention indefinitely in cases of threats to national security. The law allows the Ministry of Interior to detain persons suspected of crimes related to national security, honor, or impudence; in these cases persons detained are generally released within 24 hours or brought before a court within three days of detention. Decisions under this law are subject to appeal to the prime minister only. A provision of this law permits the prime minister to adjudicate complaints involving such detentions. The law permits a second six-month period of detention with approval from the criminal court, which may extend a detention indefinitely with review every six months.

In most cases a judge may order a suspect released, remanded to custody to await trial, held in pretrial detention pending investigation, or released on bail. Although suspects are entitled to bail (except in cases of violent crimes), bail was infrequent.

Authorities were more likely to grant citizens bail than noncitizens. Noncitizens charged with minor crimes may be released to their employer, although they may not leave the country until the case is resolved.

By law in non-security-related cases, the accused is entitled to legal representation throughout the process and prompt access to family members. There are provisions for government-funded legal counsel for indigent prisoners in criminal cases, and authorities generally honored this requirement. Authorities usually did not afford suspects detained under the Protection of Society Law and the Combating Terrorism Law access to counsel and delayed access to family members. The NHRC reported it had evidence that authorities did not refer some individuals arrested under the Protection of Society Law to the public prosecutor.

By law all suspects except those detained under the Protection of Society Law or the Combating Terrorism Law must be presented before the public prosecutor within 24 hours of arrest. If the public prosecutor finds sufficient evidence for further investigation, authorities may detain a suspect for up to 15 days with the approval of a judge, renewable for similar periods not to exceed 45 days, before charges must be filed in the courts. Judges may also extend pretrial detention for one month, renewable for one-month periods not to exceed half of the maximum punishment for the accused crime. Authorities typically followed these procedures differently for citizens than for noncitizens.

<u>Arbitrary Arrest</u>: The law prohibits arbitrary arrest and detention, and the government observed these prohibitions.

Detainee's Ability to Challenge Lawfulness of Detention before a Court: Persons arrested or detained, regardless of whether on criminal or other grounds, are entitled to challenge in court the legal basis or arbitrary nature of their detention and obtain prompt release and compensation if found to have been unlawfully detained.

Amnesty: In March the emir pardoned poet Muhammad al-Ajami, aka Ibn-al-Dheeb, and released him from prison after serving five years. Al-Ajami received a life sentence in 2011 on charges of insulting the country's former emir and inciting the public against the ruling family. A 2012 appeal reduced the penalty to 15 years.

e. Denial of Fair Public Trial

Although the constitution provides for an independent judiciary, the emir, based on recommended selections from the Supreme Judicial Council, appoints all judges, who hold their positions at his discretion. In 2015 approximately 55 percent of the judges were foreign citizens dependent on residency permits. Foreign detainees had access to the legal system, although some complained of opaque legal procedures and complications mostly stemming from language barriers. Foreign nationals did not uniformly receive translations of legal proceedings. Some employers filed successful deportation requests against employees who had pending lawsuits against them, thus denying those employees the right to a fair trial.

Trial Procedures

The law provides for the right to a fair public trial for all residents, and the judiciary generally enforced this right, except for suspects held under the Protection of Society Law and Combating Terrorism Law.

The law provides defendants the presumption of innocence, and authorities generally inform defendants promptly of the charges brought against them, except for suspects held under the Protection of Society Law and Combating Terrorism Law. In its 2015 annual report, the NHRC called for more transparent trial procedures and highlighted in verdicts issued by various courts significant typographical errors that might mar the fairness and adequacy of these verdicts. Judges give verdicts, and trials are open to the public, but the presiding judge may close the courtroom to the public if the case is deemed sensitive. The defendant may be present at his or her trial.

Defendants are entitled to choose their legal representation or accept it at public expense throughout the pretrial and trial process. In matters involving family law,

Shia and Sunni judges may apply their interpretations of sharia for their religious groups. In family law matters, a woman's testimony or worth is not weighed equally with that of a man. In some cases a woman's testimony is deemed half of a man's, and in some cases a female witness is not accepted at all.

Defense attorneys have access to government-held evidence relevant to their cases once the government files the case in court. Defendants usually have free interpretation as necessary from the moment charged through all appeals. Defendants have the right to confront and question witnesses against them and to present witnesses and evidence on their own behalf. Defendants have access to government-held evidence and have the right to confront prosecution or plaintiff witnesses and present one's own witnesses and evidence. Defendants have the opportunity to give a statement at the end of their trial. Defendants have the right to appeal a decision within 15 days, and use of the appellate process was common.

The Court of Cassation requires a fee to initiate the appeals process. In some cases courts waived fees if an appellant demonstrated financial hardship.

Political Prisoners and Detainees

There were no reports of authorities arresting or detaining individuals based upon political activity during the year.

Civil Judicial Procedures and Remedies

Civil remedies are available for those seeking damages for, or cessation of, human rights violations, but there were no cases reported during the year. The law specifies circumstances that necessitate a judge's removal from a case for conflict of interest, and authorities generally observed these laws. Individuals and organizations may not appeal adverse domestic decisions to regional human rights bodies.

f. Arbitrary or Unlawful Interference with Privacy, Family, Home, or Correspondence

The constitution and the criminal procedures code prohibit such actions, and the government generally respected these prohibitions. Police and security forces, however, reportedly monitored telephone calls, e-mails, and social media posts. The government prohibits membership in political organizations.

Citizens must obtain government permission to marry foreigners, a matter generally not granted for female citizens. Male citizens may apply for residency permits and citizenship for their foreign wives, but female citizens may apply only for residency for their foreign husbands and children, not citizenship.

Section 2. Respect for Civil Liberties, Including:

a. Freedom of Speech and Press

The constitution provides for freedom of speech and press in accordance with the law, but the government limited these rights. Self-censorship remained the primary obstacle to free speech and press.

Freedom of Speech and Expression: Citizens did not discuss sensitive political and religious issues in public forums, but these issues were discussed in private and on social media. The law prohibits residents from criticizing the emir. Members of the majority foreign population censored themselves publicly on sensitive topics. A 2015 law increases penalties for damaging, removing, or performing an action that expresses hate and contempt to the country's flag, the Gulf Cooperation Council flag, or the flag of any international organization or authority. Another law criminalizes the use of the national flag without formal permission from authorities, displaying a damaged or discolored flag, or changing the flag by adding photographs, text, or designs to it.

Press and Media Freedoms: The law includes restrictive procedures on the establishment of newspapers, closure, and confiscation of assets of a publication. It also criminalizes libel and slander, including insult to dignity. A journalist may be fined up to QAR 100,000 ($27,500) and imprisoned for a year for defamation and reporting of "false news."

Members of the ruling family or proprietors who enjoyed close ties to government officials owned all print media. Both private and government-owned television and radio reflected government views; they generally did not criticize authorities or the country's policies. The government owned and partially funded the Doha-based al-Jazeera satellite television network, which carried regional, international, and theme-based programming. It also partially funded other media outlets operating in the country. Some observers and former al-Jazeera employees alleged that the government influenced the content. On November 30, the country' s internet service providers blocked access to Doha News, a website that had received significant domestic criticism for its coverage of socially sensitive issues ranging from labor rights to homosexuality. The government did not make an official statement on the closure, but maintained that the blocking of the website was a result of registration and fund-raising violations under the law. The Doha News' editor and various human rights groups such as Amnesty International called it an "act of censorship."

Censorship or Content Restrictions: In 2015 an article from the Doha Center for Media Freedom noted, "even though the Qatari government abolished censorship in 1995, media censorship still exists in Qatar and is widely practiced in the form of self-censorship." Journalists and publishers continued to self-censor due to political and economic pressures when reporting on government policies or material deemed denigrating to Islam, the ruling family, and relations with neighboring states. The Qatar Media Corporation, the Ministry of Culture and Sports, and customs officials censored material. There were no specific reports of political censorship of foreign broadcast news media or foreign programs. The government reviewed, censored, or banned foreign newspapers, magazines, films, and books for objectionable sexual, religious, and political content.

Libel/Slander Laws: Laws restrict the publication of information that could incite the overthrow of the regime or harm supreme state interests; slander the emir or heir apparent; report official secret agreements; include defamation of one of the Abrahamic faiths or blasphemy; prejudice heads of state or disturb relations; harm the national currency or the economic situation; violate the dignity of persons, the proceedings of investigations, and prosecutions in relation to family status; or defame the state or endanger its safety.

National Security: In some cases, courts ordered news outlets to refrain from covering sensitive trials.

Internet Freedom

The maximum punishments for violations of cybercrime law are up to three years in prison and a fine of 500,000 QAR ($137,500). The law prohibits any online activity that threatens the safety of the state, its general order, and its local or international peace. It also criminalizes the spread of "false news," forces internet providers to block objectionable content, and bans the publication of personal or family information, even if true. Amnesty International assessed this law to pose a serious threat to freedom of expression.

The law requires internet service providers to block objectionable content based on a request from judicial entities. Internet providers are also obligated to maintain long-term electronic records and traffic data for the government. The government-controlled internet service provider Ooredoo restricted the expression of views via the internet and censored the internet for political, religious, and pornographic content through a proxy server, which monitored and blocked websites, e-mail, and chat rooms. Users who believed authorities had censored a site mistakenly could submit the website address to have the site reviewed for suitability; there were no reports that any websites were unblocked based on this procedure. The Ministry of Transportation and Communication is responsible for monitoring and censoring objectionable content on the internet.

Internet access was widespread and more than 96 percent of households were connected to the internet, according to a 2014 UN report.

Academic Freedom and Cultural Events

The constitution provides for freedom of expression and scientific research. Instructors at Qatar University noted that they often exercised self-censorship. Instructors at foreign-based universities operating in the country, however, reported they generally enjoyed academic freedom. There were occasional government restrictions on cultural events, and some groups organizing cultural events reported they exercised self-censorship. Authorities censored books, films, and internet sites for political, religious, and sexual content and for vulgar and obscene language.

b. Freedom of Peaceful Assembly and Association

Freedom of Assembly

The constitution provides for freedom of assembly, but this right is restricted by law, including the General Assembly and Demonstration Law and the Associations and Private Institutions Law. Noncitizens are also exempt from the constitutional protections on freedom of assembly. Organizers for a public meeting must meet a number of restrictions and conditions and obtain approval from the Ministry of Interior to acquire a permit. Religious groups are required to register with the government; however, although groups that worship in private have not been prosecuted.

Freedom of Association

The constitution provides for the right to form groups, defined by the law as professional associations and private institutions, but the government significantly limited this right. Noncitizens are exempt from the constitutional protections on freedom of association. There were no reports of attempts to organize politically. There were no organized political parties, and authorities prohibited politically oriented associations. The government prohibits professional associations and private institutions from engaging in political matters or affiliating internationally. Civil society organizations must obtain approval from the Ministry of Administrative Development, Labor, and Social Affairs, which may deny their establishment if it deems them a threat to the public interest. Twenty-six professional and private organizations existed.

Administrative obstacles, including the slow pace of procedures required to form professional associations and private institutions, and strict conditions on their establishment, management, and function, restricted their recognition. The minister of administrative development, labor, and social affairs must approve applications, and the number of noncitizens cannot exceed 20 percent of the total membership without approval by the ministerial cabinet.

Professional societies must pay QAR 50,000 ($13,750) in licensing fees and QAR 10,000 ($2,750) in annual fees, and have QAR 10 million ($2.75 million) in capital funds. Private institutions must also have QAR 10 million ($2.75 million) in capital funds, but the Council of Ministers may waive this requirement. Registrations expire after three years, and an association must reregister.

Informal organizations, such as community support groups and activity clubs, operated without registration, but they may not engage in activities deemed political.

c. Freedom of Religion

See the Department of State's *International Religious Freedom Report* at www.state.gov/religiousfreedomreport/.

d. Freedom of Movement, Internally Displaced Persons, Protection of Refugees, and Stateless Persons

The constitution provides for freedom of movement within the country, foreign travel, emigration, and repatriation, but the government did not fully respect these rights. The government cooperated with the Office of the UN High Commissioner for Refugees to assist internally displaced persons, refugees, returning refugees, asylum seekers, stateless persons, and other persons of concern although it is not a signatory of the Convention Relating to the Status of Refugees or its Protocol.

In-country Movement: Restrictions on in-country movement for citizens concerned sensitive military, oil, and industrial installations. Although there was less emphasis on setting and enforcing "family-only times" at entertainment areas in Doha, several local malls and markets continued to restrict access to certain areas to foreign workers on weekends and those dressed "immodestly." Police also limited foreign workers' access to National Day celebrations on the main thoroughfare along Doha's waterfront.

Foreign Travel: The government prevented the travel of its citizens only when they were involved in court cases in progress. The government's sponsorship system severely restricted foreign travel for noncitizens and principally affected foreign workers.

On December 13, the government began a new system for requesting exit from the country. The new procedure requires that the government make a decision on whether to allow noncitizens to leave the country within 72 hours after an employee claims an employer failed to grant permission to leave. Government officials stated publicly that employees should be able to leave the country free from interference, unless blocked by a court order or an outstanding debt. The law prohibits the practice of employers withholding workers' passports and increases penalties for employers who continue to do so, but noncitizen community leaders and officials from labor-exporting countries confirmed it remained a common problem with insufficient enforcement.

Citizenship: The law allows for the revocation of citizenship. There were no reported cases of citizenship revocation during the year.

Protection of Refugees

Access to Asylum: The law does not explicitly provide for the granting of asylum or refugee status, but occasionally the government accepted such individuals as "guests" on a temporary basis. The government legally classified the small number of persons granted residence on humanitarian grounds as visitors. The government provided housing and education to these de facto refugees.

Stateless Persons

Citizenship derives solely from the father, and Qatari women cannot transmit citizenship to their noncitizen spouse or children. A woman must obtain permission from authorities before marrying a foreign national but does not lose citizenship upon marriage.

According to the NHRC, approximately 2,000 stateless bidoon residents in the country suffered some social discrimination. The bidoon were able to register for public services such as education and health care.

The law allows long-term residents to apply for citizenship after living in the country for 25 consecutive years, but the government rarely approved citizenship applications, which were reportedly capped at 50 per year. Restrictions and uneven application of the law prevented stateless persons from acquiring citizenship.

Section 3. Freedom to Participate in the Political Process

The constitution does not provide citizens the ability to choose their government in free and fair period elections held by secret ballot and based on universal and equal suffrage. The government did not allow the formation of political parties or opposition groups. The emir exercises full executive powers, including the appointment of cabinet members. The Shura Council, whose members the emir appointed, plays an advisory role only. In July the emir issued a decree extending the term of the appointed Shura Council by three years.

The constitutional provisions for electing two-thirds of the body and initiation of legislation by the Shura Council remain unimplemented. The strong influence of family and conservative tribal traditions have limited support for democratic reform.

Elections and Political Participation

Recent Elections: In May 2015 citizens elected the 29 members of the fourth Central Municipal Council, including two women, to four-year terms. The council advises the minister of municipality and urban affairs on local public services. Foreign diplomatic missions noted no apparent irregularities or fraud in the elections, although voter registration was lower than authorities expected.

<u>Political Parties and Political Participation</u>: The government did not permit the organization of political parties, and there were no attempts to form them during the year. Voting is open to all citizens who are at least 18 years old, including those who have been naturalized for at least 15 years; members of the armed services or employees of the Ministry of Interior may not vote.

<u>Participation of Women and Minorities</u>: Although traditional attitudes and societal roles continued to limit women' s participation in politics, women served in various roles in public office, such as Minister of Public Health, chair of the Qatar Foundation, head of the General Authority for Museums, permanent representative to the United Nations, and ambassadors to Croatia and the Holy See. Two women served on the Central Municipal Council, and there were five female judges on the Court of First Instance. Noncitizen residents are banned from participating in political affairs, although they serve as judges and staffers at government ministries.

Section 4. Corruption and Lack of Transparency in Government

The law provides criminal penalties for official corruption, and the government generally implemented these laws effectively. There were reports, however, of government corruption during the year. In November 2015 the emir issued a new law increasing penalties for corrupt officials. In October the emit signed new legislation giving the State Audit Bureau more financial authority and independence and allowing it to publish parts of its findings, provided confidential information is removed, something it was not previously empowered to do. Local media reported the court system prosecuted at least 14 cases of embezzlement during the year.

<u>Financial Disclosure</u>: There are no legal requirements for public officials to disclose their income and assets, and they did not do so.

<u>Public Access to Information</u>: The law does not provide for public access to government information beyond the requirement that the government publish laws in the official gazette. Information on the government, such as up-to-date budget figures, expenditures, or draft laws, was generally not available.

Section 5. Governmental Attitude Regarding International and Nongovernmental Investigation of Alleged Violations of Human Rights

Several quasi-governmental organizations are under a single entity, Qatar Foundation, which is ultimately responsible to the legally designated founder, the emir's mother, Sheikha Moza bint Nasser al-Misnid. These organizations cooperated with the government, rarely (with the exception of the NHRC) criticized it, and did not engage in political activity. Some nongovernmental organizations (NGOs) focus on labor rights and often work in conjunction with the government.

Researchers from other NGOs such as Amnesty International and Human Rights Watch continued to visit and report on the country with limited interference from authorities. Several NGO employees reported that authorities initially prevented them from entering the country before ultimately relenting and allowing them to continue their work.

<u>Government Human Rights Bodies</u>: The NHRC investigated local human rights conditions. A 2015 law regulated the work of the NHRC, granting the committee "full independence" in practicing its activities and provided immunity to the committee's members. The NHRC typically handled petitions by liaising with government institutions to ensure a timely resolution to disputes.

Section 6. Discrimination, Societal Abuses, and Trafficking in Persons

Women

<u>Rape and Domestic Violence</u>: The law criminalizes rape. Spousal rape is not explicitly criminalized, but a woman may file a complaint. The penalty for rape is life imprisonment, regardless of the age or gender of the victim. If the perpetrator is a relative, teacher, guardian, or caregiver of the victim, the penalty is death. The government enforced the law against rape, but victims generally feared social stigma and underreported the crime.

No specific law criminalizes domestic violence. According to the NHRC, authorities may prosecute domestic violence as "general" violence under the criminal law. According to the Protection and Social Rehabilitation Center shelter (PSRC), rape and domestic violence against women continued to be a problem. In the past police treated domestic violence as a private family matter rather than a criminal matter and were reluctant to investigate or prosecute reports. There were neither arrests nor convictions for family domestic violence among citizens publicized in the press, although there were reports of cases involving noncitizens. Police maintained a women-only division to receive in-person complaints but due to conservative social mores did not enter homes without permission of the male head of household. In 2015 the PSRC reported receiving 397 cases of domestic abuses against women, including 130 citizens and 267 noncitizens. Foreign embassies had no data on sexual abuse of their citizens in the country.

Resources for female victims of violence were limited. The Supreme Council for Family Affairs (SCFA) operated a shelter in Doha under the supervision of the PSRC to accommodate up to 25 cases of abused women and children. The shelter provided a variety of services, including financial assistance, legal aid, and psychological counseling. The PSRC also opened an office in the Attorney General's Office to improve case coordination with the public prosecutor.

Sexual Harassment: Sexual harassment is illegal and carries penalties of imprisonment or fines. In some cases sponsors sexually harassed and mistreated foreign domestic servants. In a 2014 report, the UN Committee on the Elimination of Discrimination against Women expressed "deep concern" at the "high prevalence of domestic and sexual violence against women and girls, including women migrant domestic workers." Many domestic servants did not press charges due to fear of losing their jobs. During the year the PSRC reported seven cases of sexual harassment. When the domestic employees brought harassment to the attention of authorities, the employees were occasionally deported, and the government did not file charges against the employer.

Reproductive Rights: There were no reports of government interference in the rights of married couples to decide the number, spacing, and timing of their children; manage their reproductive health; and have access to the information and means to do so, free from discrimination, coercion, or violence. Unmarried individuals who reported pregnancies risked prosecution by authorities for extramarital sexual relations.

According to 2015 estimates by the UN Population Fund, only 37 percent of citizen women ages 15-49 used a modern method of contraceptive. The Eastern Mediterranean Health Journal noted that the top three reasons for not using any family planning method was the desire for more children, potential side effects, and objections raised by husbands.

Discrimination: The constitution asserts equality between citizens in rights and responsibilities, but social and legal discrimination against women persisted. For example, the housing law, which governs the government housing system, discriminates against women married to noncitizen men and against divorced women. The law requires five years of residency from the date of divorce before female citizens may obtain their housing entitlement. Women married to noncitizens or to bidoon must reside in the country with their husbands for five consecutive years before applying for the housing benefit.

Under the Nationality Law, female citizens face legal discrimination, since they are unable to obtain or transmit citizenship to their noncitizen husbands and to children born from a marriage to a noncitizen.

In order to receive maternity care, a woman must have a marriage certificate. The law requires childbirth outside of the home and also requires that births be registered with the name of the hospital or location where the birth took place.

Traditions of sharia also significantly disadvantage women in family, property, and inheritance law and in the judicial system generally. For example, a non-Muslim wife does not have the automatic right to inherit from her Muslim husband. She receives an inheritance only if her husband wills her a portion of his estate, and even then she is eligible to receive only one-third of the total estate. The proportion that women inherit depends upon their relationship to the deceased; in the cases of siblings, sisters inherit only one-half as much as their brothers. In cases of divorce, young children usually remain with the mother, regardless of her religion, unless she is found to be unfit. Women who are granted guardianship over their children by law receive their financial rights and associated right of residence.

Women may attend court proceedings and represent themselves, but a male relative generally represented them. In cases involving financial transactions, the testimony of two women equals that of one man. In family law matters, a woman's testimony is not weighed equally to that of a man. In some cases a woman's testimony is deemed half that of a man's, and in some cases a female witness is not accepted at all.

A non-Muslim woman is not required to convert to Islam upon marriage to a Muslim, but many did so. The government documents children born to a Muslim father as Muslims. Men may prevent adult female family members from leaving the country, but only by seeking and securing a court order. There were no reports that the government prevented women over age 18 from traveling abroad.

Women typically received equal pay for equal work, but they often lacked access to decision-making positions. According to a report by investment firm al-Masah Capital, in 2015, 6 percent of women reported owning their own company while 32 percent reported their intention to start their own business. While labor force participation for women was 59 percent, only 7 percent of legislators, senior officials, and managers, and 0.3 percent of board members were women. Men typically received more generous packages than women because of their positions.

There was no specialized government office devoted to women's equality.

Children

Birth registration: Children derive citizenship from the father. The government generally registered all births immediately. Female citizens cannot transmit citizenship to their noncitizen husbands or children.

Education: Education is free and compulsory for all citizens through age 18 or nine years of education, whichever comes first. Education is compulsory for noncitizen children, but they pay a nominal fee. Noncitizen residents on work visas generally must send their children to local private schools. Islamic instruction is compulsory for Muslims attending state-sponsored schools.

Child Abuse: There were limited cases of reported child abuse, family violence, and sexual abuse. In 2015 the PSRC reported that it received 389 cases involving abuse of children involving 174 citizens and 215 noncitizens.

Early and Forced Marriage: By law the minimum age for marriage is 18 years for boys and 16 years for girls. The law does not permit marriage of persons below these ages except in conformity with religious and cultural norms. These norms include the need to obtain consent from the legal guardian to ensure that both prospective partners consent to the union and apply for permission from a competent court. Underage marriage was very rare.

Sexual Exploitation of Children: No specific law sets a minimum age for consensual sex. The law prohibits sex outside of marriage. In the criminal law, the penalty for sexual relations with a person younger than 16 years is life imprisonment. If the individual is the relative, guardian, caretaker, or servant of the victim, the penalty is death; there were no reports this sentence was ever implemented. No specific law prohibits child pornography because all pornography is prohibited, but the law specifically criminalizes the commercial sexual exploitation of children.

The PSRC conducted awareness campaigns on the rights of the child and maintained a special hotline in Arabic and English that allowed both citizen and noncitizen children to call with questions and concerns ranging from school, health, and psychological problems to sexual harassment. The hotline operated in conjunction with the family abuse hotline.

International Child Abductions: The country is not a party to the 1980 Hague Convention on the Civil Aspects of International Child Abduction. See the Department of State's *Annual Report on International Parental Child Abduction* at report on compliance at travel.state.gov/content/childabduction/en/legal/compliance.html.

Anti-Semitism

The country does not have an indigenous Jewish community. In June the daily *al-Sharq* published an anti-Semitic poem titled "The Plot of the Jews" that accused Jews of spreading corruption and plotting against Muslims.

Trafficking in Persons

See the Department of State's *Trafficking in Persons Report* at www.state.gov/j/tip/rls/tiprpt/.

Persons with Disabilities

The law prohibits discrimination against--and requires the allocation of resources for--persons with physical, sensory, intellectual, and mental disabilities in employment, education, access to health care, the judicial system, and other government services or other areas. Information on patterns of abuse at education facilities, mental health facilities, or prisons was not available. The government is charged with acting on complaints from individuals, and the NHRC and enforcing compliance.

Private and independent schools generally provided most of the required services for students with disabilities, but government schools did not. Few public buildings met the required standards of accessibility for persons with disabilities, and new buildings generally did not comply with standards. The SCFA is responsible for verifying compliance with the rights and provisions mandated under the law, but compliance was not effectively enforced.

Acts of Violence, Discrimination, and Other Abuses Based on Sexual Orientation and Gender Identity

Lesbian, gay, bisexual, transgender, and intersex (LGBTI) persons faced discrimination under the law and in practice. The law prohibits same-sex sexual conduct between men but does not explicitly prohibit same-sex relations between women. Under the law a man convicted of having sexual relations with a boy younger than 16 years is subject to a sentence of life in prison. A man convicted of having same-sex sexual relations with a man 16 years of age or older may receive a sentence of seven years in prison. Data was not maintained on how many such cases were brought to court.

There were no public reports of violence against LGBTI persons. LGBTI individuals largely hid their sexual preferences in public due to an underlying pattern of discrimination toward LGBTI persons based on the country' s cultural, religious, and societal values. There were no government efforts to address potential discrimination nor are there antidiscrimination laws.

Due to social and religious conventions, there were no LGBTI organizations, gay pride marches, or gay rights advocacy events. Information was not available on official or private discrimination in employment, occupation, housing, statelessness, or access to education or health care based on sexual orientation and gender identity. Victims of such discrimination were unlikely to come forth and complain because of the potential for further harassment or discrimination.

HIV and AIDS Social Stigma

There was discrimination against HIV-positive patients. Authorities deported foreigners found to be HIV positive upon arrival. Mandatory medical examinations required for residents diagnosed their conditions. Since health screenings are required for nonresidents to obtain work visas, some HIV-positive persons were denied work permits prior to arrival. The government quarantined HIV-positive citizens and provided treatment for them.

Section 7. Worker Rights

a. Freedom of Association and the Right to Collective Bargaining

The law does not adequately protect the right of workers to form and join independent unions, conduct legal strikes, and bargain collectively, which made the exercise of these rights difficult. The law provides workers in private sector enterprises that have 100 citizen workers age 18 and older a limited right to organize, strike, and bargain collectively. The law does not prohibit antiunion discrimination or provide for reinstatement of workers fired for union activity.

The law excludes government employees, noncitizens, domestic workers, drivers, nurses, cooks, gardeners, casual workers, workers employed at sea, and most workers employed in agriculture and grazing from the right to join worker committees or the national union, effectively banning these workers from organizing, bargaining collectively, or striking.

In organizations with more than 30 workers, the law permits the establishment of "joint committees" with an equal number of worker and management representatives to deal with a limited number of workplace problems. Foreign workers may be members of joint labor-management committees. The law offers a means to file collective disputes. If disputes are not settled internally between the employees and employer, the Ministry of Administrative Development, Labor, and Social Affairs may mediate a solution.

The law requires approval by the Ministry of Administrative Development, Labor, and Social Affairs for worker organizations to affiliate with groups outside the country. The government did not respect freedom of association and the right to collective bargaining.

For those few workers covered by the law protecting the right to collective bargaining, the government circumscribed the right through its control over the rules and procedures of the bargaining and agreement processes. The labor code allows for only one trade union, the General Union of Workers of Qatar (General Union), which was composed of general committees for workers in various trades or industries. Trade or industry committees were composed of worker committees at the individual firm level. The General Union was not a functioning entity.

Employees could not freely practice collective bargaining, and there were no workers under collective bargaining contracts. While rare, when labor unrest occurred, mostly involving the country' s overwhelmingly foreign workforce, the government reportedly responded by dispatching large numbers of police to the work sites or labor camps involved; the strikes generally ended peacefully after these shows of force. In most cases the government summarily deported the workers' leaders and organizers. International labor NGOs were able to send researchers into the country under the sponsorship of academic institutions and quasi-governmental organizations such as the NHRC.

Although the law recognizes the right to strike for some workers, restrictive conditions made the likelihood of a legal strike extremely remote. The law requires approval for a strike by three-fourths of the General Committee of the workers in the trade or the industry, and potential strikers also must exhaust a lengthy dispute resolution procedure before a lawful strike may be called. Civil servants and domestic workers do not have the right to strike; the law also prohibits strikes at public utilities and health or security service facilities, including the gas, petroleum, and transportation sectors. The Complaint Department of the Ministry of Administrative Development, Labor, and Social Affairs in coordination with the Ministry of Interior must preauthorize all strikes, including approval of the time and place.

b. Prohibition of Forced or Compulsory Labor

The law prohibits all forms of forced or compulsory labor. International media and human rights organizations alleged numerous abuses against foreign workers, including forced or compulsory labor, withheld wages, unsafe working conditions, poor living accommodations, employers who routinely confiscated worker passports, and a sponsorship system that gave employers inordinate control of workers.

The government made efforts to prevent and eliminate forced labor, although the restrictive sponsorship system left some migrant workers vulnerable to exploitation. In October 2015 the government issued Law No. 21 of 2015, which reforms the s residency permitting and labor sponsorship systems for foreign employees. The new law, which came into force on December 13, allows employees to switch employers at the end of their contract, which can be up to five years, without the permission of their employer--a current driver of forced labor practices. Employees may also switch in cases of failure to pay, violation of contract, mutual agreement, filing of a legal case in court, and bankruptcy or death of employer. The government also inaugurated several new government-funded labor accommodation sites designed to replace unsafe temporary housing for migrant workers. The government arrested and prosecuted individuals for suspected labor law violations; two cases each of forced labor and bonded labor were before courts in 2014. As of November no forced labor cases were referred to the courts through the Labor Relations Department at the Ministry of Administrative Development, Labor, and Social Affairs. In July the Labor

Inspection Department at the same ministry announced that it shut down 60 work sites for violating a ministerial decision setting the working hours for laborers exposed to the sun during the summer. The Ministry of Administrative Development, Labor, and Social Affairs, the Ministry of Interior, and the NHRC conducted training sessions for migrant laborers to educate them on their rights in the country. The three entities also printed and distributed pamphlets that included pertinent articles of the labor and sponsorship laws in multiple languages to educate migrant workers on their rights. To combat the problem of late and unpaid wages, in February 2015 the government issued a law mandating electronic payment to all employees subject to the labor law. By November 2015, the government required all employers to open bank accounts for their employees and pay wages electronically through a system subject to audits by a new inspection division at the Ministry of Administrative Development, Labor, and Social Affairs. Employers who failed to pay their workers faced penalties of QAR 2,000-6,000 ($550-$1,650) per case and possible prison sentences.

There were continuing indications of forced labor, especially in the construction and domestic labor sectors, which disproportionately affected migrant workers. Exorbitant recruitment fees incurred abroad entrapped many workers in long-term debt, making them more vulnerable to exploitation for forced labor under the restrictive sponsorship system. Some foreign workers who voluntarily entered the country to work had their passports and pay withheld, were refused exit permits, and worked under conditions to which they had not agreed. In March an Amnesty International report stated that they interviewed 234 workers, all of whose passports were confiscated by the employer. Law No. 21 of 2015 reduced exit barriers but did not eliminate them.

Also see the Department of State's *Trafficking in Persons Report* at www.state.gov/j/tip/rls/tiprpt/.

c. Prohibition of Child Labor and Minimum Age for Employment

The law sets the minimum age for employment at 16 years and stipulates that minors between the ages of 16 and 18 years may work with parental or guardian permission. Minors may not work more than six hours a day or more than 36 hours a week. Employers must provide the Ministry of Administrative Development, Labor, and Social Affairs with the names and occupations of their minor employees and obtain permission from the Ministry of Education and Higher Education to hire a minor. The ministry may prohibit the employment of minors in jobs judged dangerous to their health, safety, or morals. The government generally enforced relevant laws effectively, and child labor rarely occurred.

d. Discrimination with Respect to Employment and Occupation

The constitution prohibits discrimination based on sex, race, language, and religion, but not political opinion, national origin, social origin, disability, sexual orientation, age, or HIV-positive status. Local custom, however, outweighed government enforcement of nondiscrimination laws, and legal, cultural, and institutional discrimination existed against women, noncitizens, and foreign workers. The government prohibited lower paid male workers from residing in specific "family" residential zones throughout the country. The government discriminated against noncitizens in employment, education, housing, and health services (see section 6).

The law requires reserving 2 percent of jobs in government agencies and public institutions for persons with disabilities, and most government entities appeared to conform to this law. Private sector businesses employing a minimum of 25 persons are also required to hire persons with disabilities as 2 percent of their staff. Employers who violate these employment provisions are subject to fines of up to QAR 20,000 ($5,500). There were no reports of violations of the hiring quota requirement during the year.

e. Acceptable Conditions of Work

There is no minimum wage. The law requires equal pay for equal work in the private sector. The labor law provides for a 48-hour workweek with a 24-hour rest period and paid annual leave days. The law requires premium pay for overtime and prohibits excessive compulsory overtime. Employees who work more than 48 hours per week or 36 hours per week during the month of Ramadan are entitled to an overtime pay supplement of at least 25 percent. The government sets occupational health and safety standards including restrictions on working during the hottest hours of the day during the summer and general restrictions related to temperature during the rest of the day as well. The labor law and provisions for acceptable conditions of work do not apply to workers in the public sector or agriculture, or to domestic workers. Poverty among citizens was very low, and the government did not track poverty statistics among migrant workers.

Responsibility for laws related to acceptable conditions of work fell primarily to the Ministry of Administrative Development, Labor, and Social Affairs as well as the Ministry of Energy and Industry and the Ministry of Public Health. The government did not effectively enforce standards in all sectors; working conditions for citizens were generally adequate, because government agencies and the major private sector companies employing them generally followed the relevant laws. Enforcement problems were in part due to insufficient training and lack of personnel. As of August there were approximately 380 inspectors in the Ministry of Administrative Development, Labor, and Social Affairs.

The government took limited action to prevent violations and improve working conditions. The Ministry of Administrative Development, Labor, and Social Affairs received 6,111 disputes in 2015, 886 of which were resolved by labor courts. From January to September of this year, the Ministry of Interior assisted in moving 1,784 workers to new employers in response to complaints against their employers such as failure to pay or filing of a criminal case. The labor courts referred a limited number of labor complaints to the criminal courts, but statistics were not publicly available. In October the government announced it was forming several new worker dispute committees chaired by judges and designed to process new worker complaints within three weeks.

The Labor Inspection Department conducted monthly and random inspections of foreign worker camps. When inspectors found the camps to be below minimum standards, the operators received a warning, and authorities ordered them to remedy the violations within one month. For example, inspectors reportedly checked companies' payrolls and health and safety practices, returning after one month to ensure any recommended changes were made. If a company did not remedy the violations, the Ministry of Administrative Development, Labor, and Social Affairs blacklisted the company and on occasion referred the matter to the public prosecutor for action.

Fear of penalties such as blacklisting appeared to have had some effect as a deterrent to some labor law violations. Blacklisting is an administrative hold on a company or individual that freezes government services such as processing new visa applications from the firms. Firms must pay a QAR 3,000 ($825) fine to be removed from the list--even if the dispute is resolved--and the ministry reserves the right to keep companies on the list after the fine is paid as a punitive measure. The ministry reportedly blacklisted 34,662 firms as of October. The Ministry of Administrative Development, Labor, and Social Affairs announced that in August it also stripped the licenses of 15 recruitment agencies for violation of labor laws.

As of October inspectors conducted 32,718 observations of work and labor housing sites. Inspectors found that 58.9 percent of companies received no violations, 35.4

percent received warnings, and 5.7 percent received a violation report or penalty, although some rights workers questioned the quality of the audits done at such sites claiming their own work revealed far more violations. Violators faced penalties of up to QAR 6,000 ($1,650) and 30 days' imprisonment in the most serious cases, but labor observers reported that most safety and health violations were handled through administrative fines or blacklisting. The ministry maintained an office in Doha's industrial area, where most unskilled foreign workers resided, to receive complaints about worker safety or nonpayment of wages.

Violations of wage, overtime, and safety and health standards were relatively common, especially in sectors employing foreign workers, in which working conditions were often poor. In November 2015, the government implemented the new Wage Protection System, a law mandating that employers pay their employees electronically to provide a digital audit trail for the Ministry of Administrative Development, Labor, and Social Affairs to inspect. Employers who failed to pay their workers faced penalties of QAR 2,000-6,000 ($550-$1,650) per employee and possible prison sentences. Violations of the Wage Protection System resulted in the prosecution of 385 corporations during the year. By law employees have a right to remove themselves from situations that endangered their health or safety without jeopardy to their employment, but authorities did not effectively provide protection to employees exercising this right. Employers often ignored working hour restrictions and other laws with respect to domestic workers and unskilled laborers, the majority of whom were foreigners.

Reports from news outlets and human rights organizations alleged that some employers did not pay many workers for their overtime or annual leave. While the practice continued, the frequency of these abuses was reportedly declining. Employers housed many unskilled foreign laborers in cramped, dirty, and hazardous conditions, often without running water, electricity, or adequate food. During the year two new high-end health centers devoted to caring for laborers were built. In October 2015 the government opened up its first labor-housing city, which has a 70,000-person capacity. Throughout the year international media alleged some abusive working conditions existed, including work-related deaths of young foreign workers, especially in the construction sector.

Domestic workers often faced unacceptable working conditions. Many such workers frequently worked seven days a week and more than 12 hours a day with few or no holidays, no overtime pay, and limited means to redress grievances. Some employers denied domestic workers food or access to a telephone, according to news reports and foreign embassy officials.

The consensus among international NGOs was that foreign workers faced legal obstacles and lengthy legal processes that prevented them from seeking redress for violations and exploitative conditions. Noncitizen community leaders also highlighted migrant workers' continued hesitation to report their plight due to fear of reprisals.